Magic

HANDBOOK

MAGICAL ILLUSIONS

Jon Tremaine

QED Publishing

Editor: Michael Downey
Designer: Louise Downey
Illustrator: Mark Turner for
         Beehive Illustrations

Copyright © QED Publishing 2010
First published in the UK in 2010 by
QED Publishing
A Quarto Group Company
226 City Road
London EC1V 2TT

www.qed-publishing.co.uk

Picture credits
Corbis Lawrence Manning 13
Getty Images Adam Gault 27
Shutterstock Andrejs Pidjass 11, 3dfoto 17, spiller 29
Michael Vincent 25

A catalogue record for this book is available from the
British Library.

ISBN 978 1 84835 446 3

Printed in China

Contents

Amazing illusions	4
Simple thimble	6
Sense of direction	8
Upside-down card	10
Safety first	12
One-way street	14
Crazy shoelaces	16
Jumpin' Joker	18
Last straw	20
Bangle wangle	22
Double your money	24
Mind reading	26
Magical clock	28
Coin in pocket	30
Elastic arm	32

Magicians use props to create their magical illusions. Usually, these are simple everyday objects. With just some string, a drinking straw, a thimble, safety pins and shoelaces you can perform some great tricks!

② Difficulty rating

The magic tricks get harder throughout the book (except on page 32), so each trick has been given a rating. One is the easiest and seven is the hardest. The most difficult tricks will take a bit of practice to get right, but they will be worth it!

① Preparation

Sometimes you will need to prepare something beforehand to make a trick work.

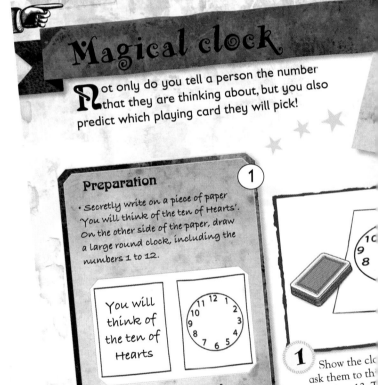

Magical clock

Not only do you tell a person the number that they are thinking about, but you also predict which playing card they will pick!

Preparation ①

• Secretly write on a piece of paper 'You will think of the ten of Hearts'. On the other side of the paper, draw a large round clock, including the numbers 1 to 12.

You will think of the ten of Hearts

• Take out the ten of Hearts from your pack and put two pencil dots on the back of it in the top left and bottom right corners. Put this card back in the pack, 13th from the top.

① Show the clo ask them to th from 1 to 12. T same number the pack and head so that y many cards th

Top
This impressi acting you c very difficul for you no

Putting on a show

An excellent magician is also a great performer. The better you are at putting on a show, then the more believable your illusions will be. Remember that props are very useful as they can help bring a trick to life.

3 Props needed...

The props you will need throughout the book.

- Bangles
- Book
- Coins
- Craft knife
- Dictionary
- Drinking straw
- Glue

- Handkerchief
- Jacket with pockets
- Magic wand
- Pack of playing cards
- Paper
- Paper bag
- Pencil

- Red shoelace
- Safety pins
- Scissors
- String
- Thimble
- White card
- Yellow shoelace

2 Say "I need 12 cards," and count off the top 12 cards, one at a time, and stack them into a little pile. This reverses the order of the cards and is important. Put the other cards aside.

3 Starting at one o'clock, go around the clock and put a card beside each number. As you do this, watch out for your card with the pencil dots in the corners. This will land on the number that your friend is thinking about! Let's assume that it lands at six o'clock.

4 Say to your friend "Please think of your number." After a few seconds, say "You are thinking of the number six and you are sitting on six cards! Am I right?" Then say "Let's see what card lies at six o'clock." Turn it over to show the ten of Hearts. Then remove all the other cards from the clock and turn over the piece of paper. Your friend will read 'You will think of the ten of Hearts'. Amazing!

▶ Dai Vernon was one of the few people who could trick the famous Harry Houdini with a card trick.

Fooling Houdini

Magician Dai Vernon (1894–1992) was known as the 'professor'. He was perhaps the most skilful playing-card magician in the history of magic. He even fooled the great Houdini when he performed his trick the 'Ambitious Card'. He repeated the trick eight times and still Houdini could not work out what Vernon was doing!

29

4 Stages and illustrations

Step-by-step instructions, as well as illustrations, will guide you through each trick.

5 Top Tip!

Hints and tips help you to perform the tricks better!

6 Famous magicians and illusions

Find out who are the most exciting and skilful magicians, and what amazing feats they have performed.

Simple thimble

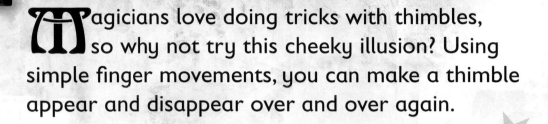

Magicians love doing tricks with thimbles, so why not try this cheeky illusion? Using simple finger movements, you can make a thimble appear and disappear over and over again.

Props needed...
* Thimble

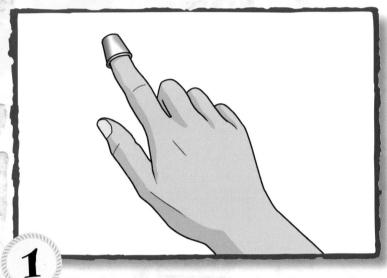

1 Fit the thimble on the first finger of your right hand.

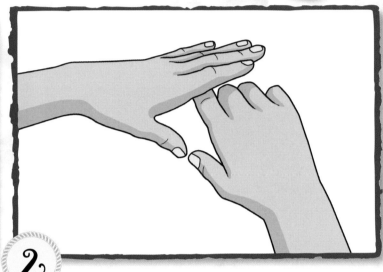

2 Cover the thimble with your open left hand so that it can't be seen.

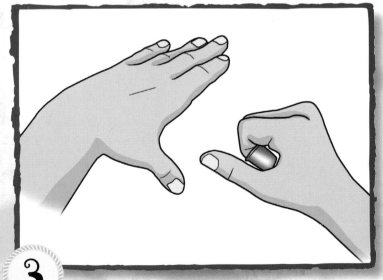

3 When the thimble is hidden, close your right hand. Keep your right hand hidden under your left hand.

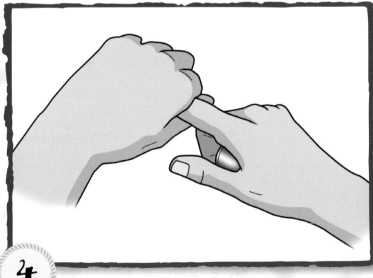

4 Hold the thimble between your right hand's second finger and thumb. As soon as you have done this, shoot your first finger forwards and grip it with the fingers of your left hand.

6

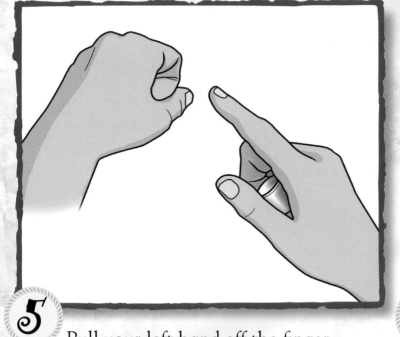

5 Pull your left hand off the finger. Your friend will think that the thimble is now in your left hand.

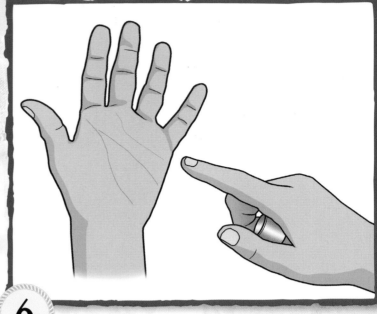

6 Wait a few seconds before you open your left hand to show your friend that the thimble has vanished!

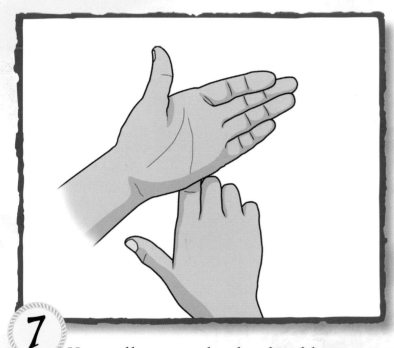

7 You will now make the thimble reappear. Hide your right fingers with your left hand. Push your right-hand first finger into the thimble and straighten it.

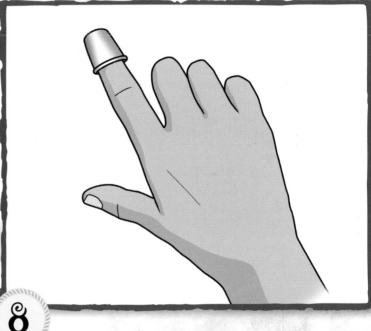

8 Take away your left hand to show that, magically, the thimble is back on the first finger of your right hand!

 Top Tip!

Some thimbles will be too large for your finger. Look around until you find one that fits your finger – not too tight, not too loose.

Sense of direction

This is an effective illusion that you can perform at any time. The only thing you will need is a clever miniature road sign, which you can keep in your pocket.

Props needed...
* Small piece of white card
* Scissors
* Glue
* Pencil

Preparation

• Draw or photocopy the road sign onto card. Then draw the arrows as shown. Fold the road sign in half along the dotted line and glue the two halves together.

• There are many ways of holding the road sign. If you hold the sign in position A in your left hand, the arrows on both sides will be pointing the same way when you turn the sign with your right-hand thumb.

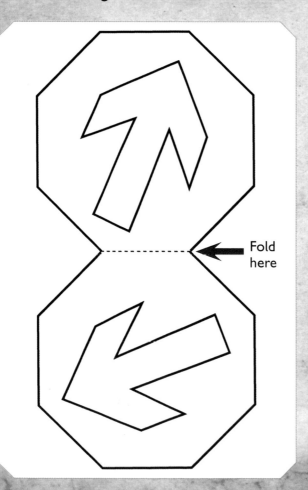

Fold here

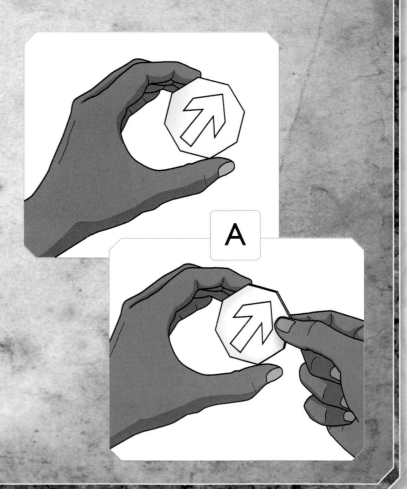

A

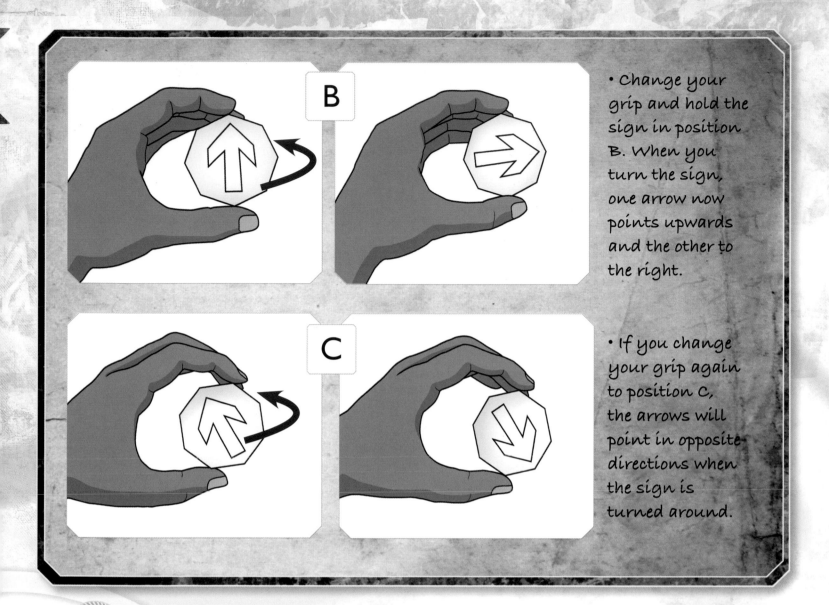

- Change your grip and hold the sign in position B. When you turn the sign, one arrow now points upwards and the other to the right.

- If you change your grip again to position C, the arrows will point in opposite directions when the sign is turned around.

1

Tell a story, such as this one, while you hold up and turn the road sign.

"I went for a drive with my father. He was the driver and I was the navigator. I told him to drive straight ahead (A), and for a while everything went fine. I wanted him to keep straight ahead (B) but he decided he wanted to go to the right.

By the time I had convinced him to go straight ahead again, I found that we had been driving around in circles (C) and finally ended up where we started.

Why don't parents ever do what they're told?"

Top Tip!

Make up a story to suit yourself. Keep things simple for the best effect. Put the road sign in your pocket when you have finished.

upside-down card

How do you find the one card that your friend chose from a pack of playing cards? It's not difficult – all you do is secretly turn the card at the bottom of the pack upside down!

Props needed...
* Pack of playing cards

Preparation

• Before you start the trick, turn over the bottom card in the pack.

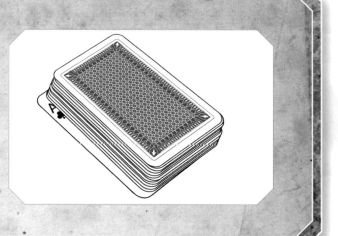

1

Spread the cards and ask your friend to take one – they must not show it to you. Keep the bottom card hidden. Once your friend has a card, tidy the pack and hold it in one hand.

Ask your friend to look at the front of the card and remember it. While they are doing this, secretly turn the pack over so that the bottom, upside-down card is now at the top. The rest of the pack is face up underneath this card.

2 Ask your friend to put their card back somewhere in the middle of the pack. They will not notice that the pack, apart from the top card, is upside down. Then say "I am going to put the pack behind my back to try and find your card without looking at the cards."

3 As soon as the cards are out of sight behind your back, turn the top card the other way so that now the only upside-down card in the pack will be your friend's card. This is somewhere in the middle of the pack.

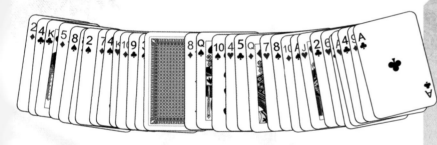

4 Bring the pack out and spread the cards across the table face up. There will be one face-down card in the middle of the cards. Ask your friend to say the name of their card. Then ask them to turn over the face-down card. This will be their card!

Clowning around

Hans Moretti's box illusion is truly amazing! The magician is first tied in chains and sealed into a box. Twelve people from the audience are asked to push long swords into the box from all sides. Is Moretti injured? No! When he comes out of the box, not only is he unharmed, he is dressed as a clown, complete with clown make-up, and is holding two doves.

◀ *How does Hans Moretti survive all these swords? It's a complete mystery!*

Safety first

L ink two ordinary safety pins together and close them up securely. Then, quick as a flash, pull them apart. Amazingly, they will magically separate while still closed.

Props needed...
* Two large safety pins

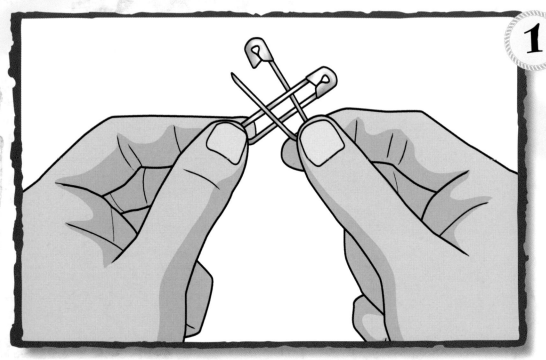

1 Link the two safety pins together by putting one open safety pin through a closed safety pin. Close the open safety pin. Then hold the two linked safety pins by their ends.

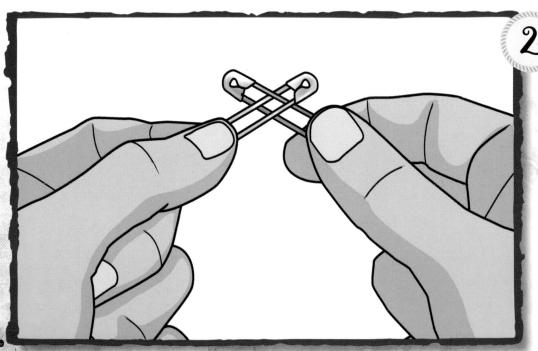

2 Make sure that the opening and non-opening bars of each pin are in the position shown in this illustration.

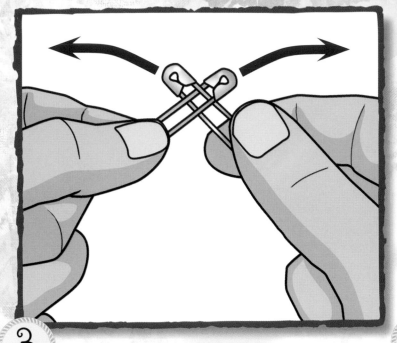

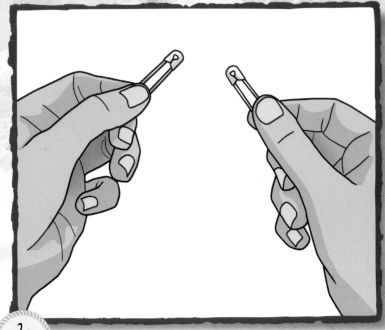

3 Once sure that you are holding the safety pins correctly, grip them tightly. Now pull sharply in opposite directions.

4 The safety pins separate, but stay closed! In fact, they open and close so quickly, that you can't see it happen. Ask someone in the audience to look at the safety pins to make sure that there was nothing wrong with them.

▲ Many magicians now perform the amazing Zig-zag Girl trick.

Zig-zag Girl

Robert Harbin's (1909–1978) Zig-zag Girl is a scary illusion. After a girl steps into a cabinet, two big blades are pushed through the cabinet, slicing the cabinet, and maybe the girl, into three pieces. When the centre section is pushed to one side, a small door is opened to show the girl's tummy. Her head and her right foot can be seen in the top and bottom sections. When the centre section is put back, the girl walks out of the cabinet unharmed!

Props needed...
* Pack of playing cards

There are 19 cards in a pack that have a 'one-way' design. These cards can be easily spotted when turned around. You can use these cards for many illusions, including this neat trick.

Preparation

• Lay out the 19 playing cards below, making sure that they are the same way up as shown. These cards look different when turned.

• Gather up the 19 cards so that they stay the same way up. Place this stack face down on a table.

• Put the Joker on top of this stack, and the other cards on the Joker.

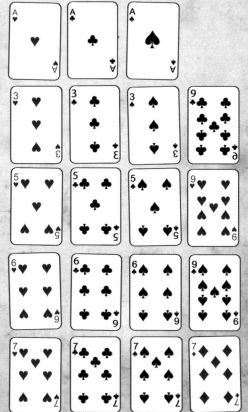

1

Tell your friend that you will not be needing all the cards from the pack. Spread out the entire pack face-up and take the 19 cards that you have secretly chosen. This is easy to do – you just have to look through the pack until you see the Joker. Put the Joker and all the cards underneath it to one side.

2

After you have let your friend shuffle the 19 cards, take them back. Then spread them out, face down, in your hands. Ask your friend to take a card, to look at it and remember it.

3

While your friend is looking at their card, secretly turn the cards you are holding around. Then ask your friend to put back their card in the pack you are holding. Also ask them to shuffle the cards again so that you cannot possibly know where it is in the pack.

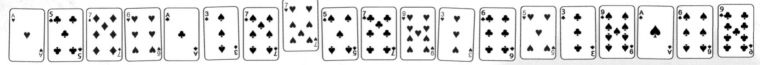

4

Take the cards back and spread them face up in a line across the table. Look for the one that is a different way up to the rest. That one is your friend's card.

5

Ask your friend to hold your wrist as you pass your hand over the line of cards. Pretend that you are using special magical powers to find the correct card. After about 10 seconds, pick up the card your friend chose and hand it to them.

Top Tip!

Some packs of cards have one-way designs on their back, such as an animal picture. Look out for packs such as these so that you can do the trick with the complete pack of 52 cards.

Crazy shoelaces

You will not believe that this trick really works until you try it for yourself. All you need are two coloured shoelaces and a magic wand. The rest is just pure magic.

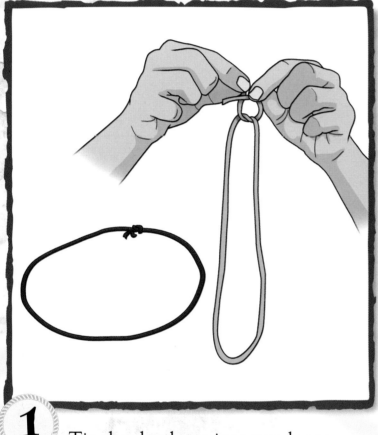

 Tie the shoelaces into two loops.

2 Thread the red loop through the other loop. Then slip the red shoelace onto the magic wand.

Top Tip!

Coloured shoelaces are sometimes not very easy to find. Fortunately, coloured string or coloured ribbons will work just as well!

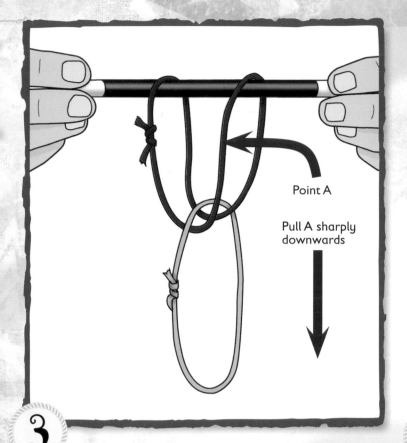

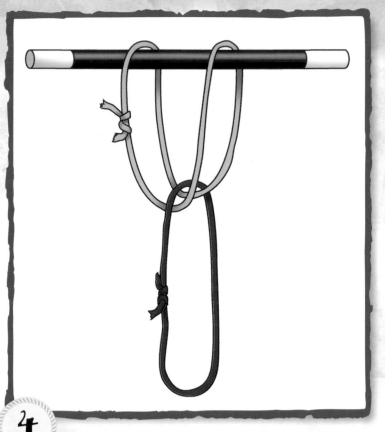

3 Ask your friend to hold onto both ends of the magic wand. Then hold the red loop at point A. Pull downwards very sharply and you will find that the two laces instantly change places.

Point A

Pull A sharply downwards

4 The yellow shoelace is now threaded onto the wand and the red shoelace now hangs loose.

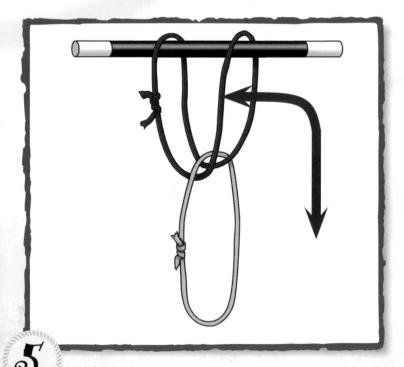

5 If you now hold the yellow shoelace at the same place that you held the red shoelace and pull, the two shoelaces will change places again!

Vanishing cards

Magician Paul Potassy's best trick involves two seated spectators who deal themselves 20 playing cards each and sit on them. Potassy then magically moves one person's 20 cards to the other person so that one person now sits on 40 cards. The cards under the other person vanish! Neither spectator has any idea how he does it.

▶ Paul Potassy's amazing card trick always delights his audiences.

Jumpin' Joker

It must be magic when a card that your friend is holding in their hand suddenly vanishes and then reappears in your pocket!

Props needed...
* Pack of playing cards
* Handkerchief
* Scissors

Preparation

• Take out the two Jokers, the King of Hearts and the King of Clubs from your pack of playing cards. Put the rest of the pack aside.

• Cut out a piece from the end of one of the Jokers. This should be 20 x 25 millimetres.

• Remove the two Kings and cut off a thin strip 1.5 millimetres wide from their long, left edge. This makes them slightly narrower.

• Put the Joker you have not cut in your pocket.

1 To do this trick, sit at a table with your friend sitting opposite you.

2 Hold the three cards in your left hand and show them to your friend. The cut part of the Joker is hidden behind the top King of Hearts.

3 Carefully close the cards up and give them to your friend to hold. Make sure that the cut end is between their thumb and first finger.

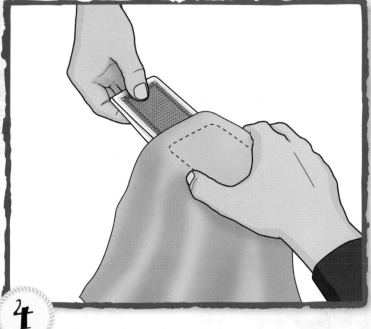

4 Say to your friend "In a moment, this is what I'm going to do." Throw the handkerchief over the cards and your friend's hand. Then grip the edges of the cards and pull the handkerchief away. This will take the Joker away in the handkerchief as it is wider than the other two cards. Your friend will not feel anything! Drop the handkerchief with the hidden Joker into your lap.

5 Now say "Hold onto the cards. I'm going to cover your hand with the handkerchief again and make the Joker jump into my pocket." Pretend that you are magically taking away the Joker from your friend and throwing it into your pocket. Remove the handkerchief and leave it on the table. Ask your friend to look for the Joker. It has gone!

6 Remove the other Joker from your pocket. Your friend will believe it jumped into your pocket as you said it would!

Top Tip!
You don't have to hurry to hide the Joker in your lap. Your friend will lift the handkerchief when looking for the Joker. That's the time to secretly slip the Joker into your pocket.

Last straw

Thread a piece of string through a drinking straw and cut both of them in half. Then, magically, restore the piece of string to its original length. You will have to practise this daring trick a few times before you try it on a friend.

Props needed...
* Drinking straw
* String, one metre long
* Scissors
* Craft knife

Preparation
• Ask an adult to cut an 8-centimetre slit along the centre of the straw.

Cut slit here

1   Pick up the straw with the slit side hidden from your friend. Thread the string through the straw.

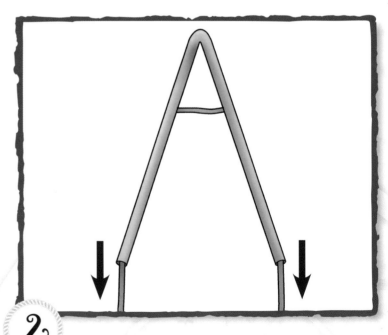

2   Fold the straw in half. At the same time, pull the two ends of the string down. This will make part of the string come through the slit in the straw.

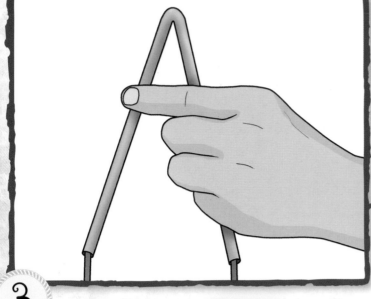

3 Hide the piece of string that has come through the straw with your left first finger and thumb.

4 Cut through the centre of the straw with the scissors. Your friend will think you are also cutting the string!

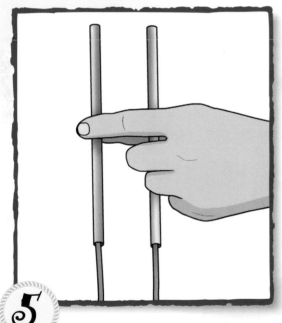

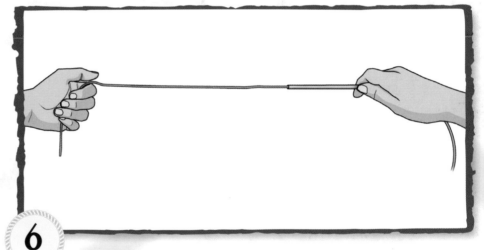

6 Hold the two cut ends of the straw together and slowly pull out the string. Amazingly, it will be one complete length of string again!

5 Hold up the two halves of the straw in your left hand. You must hide with your finger and thumb the section of string that you pulled through the slit.

Top Tip!

Keep your secret safe by quietly putting the two halves of the straw in your pocket before your friend has a chance to discover how you did this impressive trick.

Bangle wangle

This trick may have been invented by Harry Houdini, perhaps the most famous magician of all time. Here, you magically take off a bangle dangling from a piece of string tied to your wrists without undoing the knots.

Props needed...
* Two identical bangles
* Piece of string, 1.5 metres long
* Jacket with an inside pocket

Preparation

• Slip one of the bangles over your right hand and gently push it up your sleeve until it is out of sight. Keep this bangle hidden.

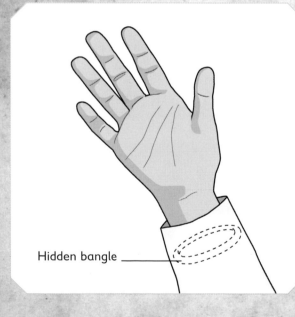

Hidden bangle

• Put the string and the other bangle on the table.

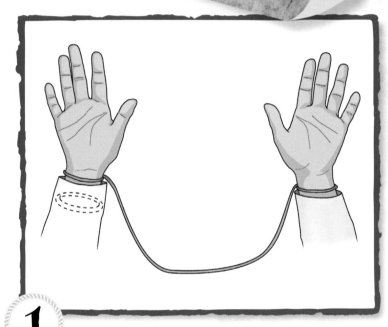

1 Ask your friend to tie the string around each of your wrists. They should leave about 40 centimetres of string between each wrist. Ask them to check that the string will not come undone and that the bangle is not broken.

Top Tip!

Practise this trick until you can do it smoothly and really quickly. The trick looks even better if you use soft white rope or a length of wide ribbon.

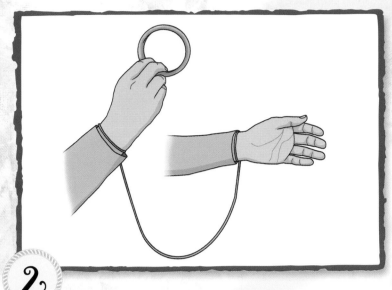

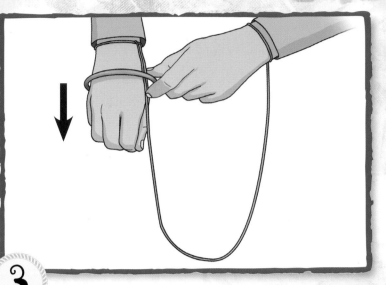

② Pick up the bangle on the table with your right hand.

③ Say "Watch!" and quickly turn your back on your friend. Put the bangle in your inside jacket pocket. Pull the hidden bangle from your sleeve, pass it over your hand and onto the string. Leave it dangling on the string.

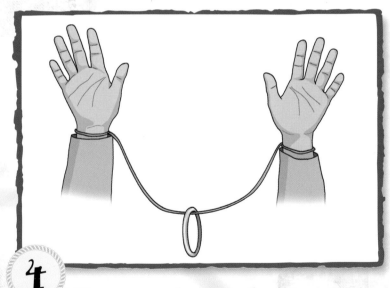

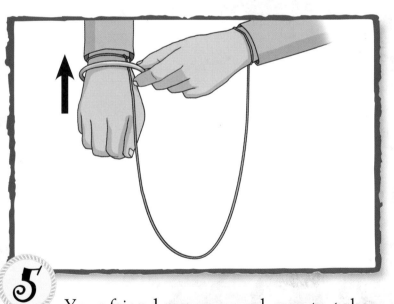

④ Turn around to face your friend. Ask them to examine the knots again to make sure that you have not secretly loosened the knots to slip the bangle onto the string.

⑤ Your friend may now ask you to take the bangle off the string. To do this, turn your back again. Then slide the bangle off the string, over your hand and wrist and hide it up your right sleeve. Reach into your inside jacket pocket with your left hand and remove the other bangle. Turn around and show your friend the loose bangle!

Double your money

How can you get rich quick? Easy! Take ten coins, tip them into an ordinary paper bag and pull out 20 coins! How is it done?

Props needed...
* 20 small coins of the same value
* Small paper bag
* Large hardback dictionary
* Magic wand

Preparation

• Open up the dictionary near its middle pages. A gap will appear between the spine and the pages at the back of the book.

• Slide 10 coins into this space and close the book. They should stay firmly in place.

1 Tell your friends that you are going to look up the word 'magic'. Pick up the dictionary and open it near the middle. Look for the word 'magic' and read the definition to your friends.

2 Say that you will now do some magic by making money double in value. Put your other ten coins on the open pages of the book and show them to your friends. Ask them to count the coins.

Practise this illusion a few times before your performance. Most dictionaries can be heavy and difficult to hold if you are not used to it.

Linking rings

Magician Michael Vincent performs the beautiful Chinese linking rings trick. First, he allows the audience to inspect closely eight, large solid-steel rings. Then, he magically passes solid metal through solid metal, linking and unlinking the rings. He joins them in pairs, threes and even into a long chain. Finally, he unlinks the rings and hands them out to the audience again.

▼ Michael Vincent is also a master of magic illusions using playing cards.

3 Ask your friends to look inside the paper bag to make sure it is empty. Then tip all the coins into the open bag. The ten coins hidden inside the dictionary's spine will also drop into the bag. Your friends won't see this happen!

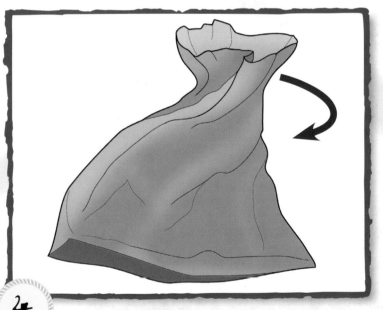

4 Put the book down and screw up the neck of the bag. Pick up your magic wand and say "Hubble bubble, make my money double." Ask a friend to open the bag and count the coins. Your friends saw you put ten coins in the bag, now there are 20!

Mind reading

Your friend uses playing cards to choose a word in a book. They do not tell you what the word is. You then use your magical skills to read their mind and write down the correct word!

Props needed...
* Reading book with more that 64 pages
* Pack of playing cards
* Paper
* Pencil

Preparation

• Arrange the pack so that the following cards are on top of the pack – a six, a four, a five and a seven. Their suit does not matter.

• Open the book at page number 64, our first two numbers. Count down to the fifth line, then count along that line until you reach the seventh word. Remember this word. Although it could be any word, let's pretend the word is 'palaces'. Close the book.

Top Tip!

Looking at the book distracts your friend's attention from what actually happened with the cards. They will have no idea that the cards that they use are the original top four cards!

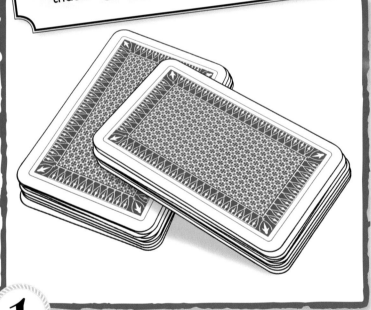

1

Ask your friend to lift off about half of the pack and put the cards to one side. As you say "We'll mark where you cut like this," lift up the remainder of the pack and place it across your friend's cards. Then hand the book to your friend and ask them to make sure that the book is real and that all the pages are different.

2 Lift off the top half of the pack and place it to one side. Point to the lower half and say "You could have cut the pack anywhere. Please take the first two cards. They're going to represent a page number in the book." Then ask them "What are they? Oh! A six and a four. Please turn to page 64 in the book." They then find the page.

3 Then say "Take the next card. Don't tell me what it is. Its number will be the line on the page. So count down to the line number." They find the line.

4 Say "Take the next card. This will show the word that I want you to think about. Count along the line until you get to the word. Don't say it out loud, just think of it." Now use your acting skills and pretend to think for about 10 seconds. Then write down the word that you have memorized – palaces – and show it to your amazed friend!

Blown away

Tony Slydini's (1900-1991) best trick was that of the disappearing tissue-paper balls. Simply by asking a member of the audience to blow on his hands, the magician would make ball after ball vanish. Although Slydini repeated the trick over and over, the spectator would have no idea how he was doing it!

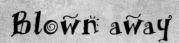

▶ Tony Slydini was a master of what is known as 'close-up magic'.

Magical clock

Not only do you tell a person the number that they are thinking about, but you also predict which playing card they will pick!

Props needed...
* Pack of playing cards
* Paper
* Pencil

Preparation

• Secretly write on a piece of paper 'You will think of the ten of Hearts'. On the other side of the paper, draw a large round clock, including the numbers 1 to 12.

You will think of the ten of Hearts

11 12 1
10   2
9   3
8   4
7 6 5

• Take out the ten of Hearts from your pack and put two pencil dots on the back of it in the top left and bottom right corners. Put this card back in the pack, 13th from the top.

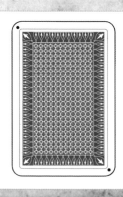

1 Show the clock to your friend and ask them to think of one of the numbers from 1 to 12. They should take out the same number of cards from the top of the pack and sit on them! Turn your head so that you cannot see how many cards they take.

Top Tip!

This impressive trick deserves every bit of acting you can come up with. Make it look very difficult. It isn't, but that is no reason for you not to take credit for great skill, is it?

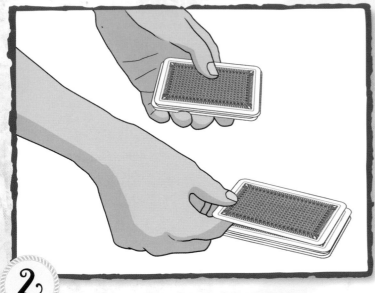

2 Say "I need 12 cards," and count off the top 12 cards, one at a time, and stack them into a little pile. This reverses the order of the cards and is important. Put the other cards aside.

3 Starting at one o'clock, go around the clock and put a card beside each number. As you do this, watch out for your card with the pencil dots in the corners. This will land on the number that your friend is thinking about! Let's assume that it lands at six o'clock.

4 Say to your friend "Please think of your number." After a few seconds, say "You are thinking of the number six and you are sitting on six cards! Am I right?" Then say "Let's see what card lies at six o'clock." Turn it over to show the ten of Hearts. Then remove all the other cards from the clock and turn over the piece of paper. Your friend will read 'You will think of the ten of Hearts'. Amazing!

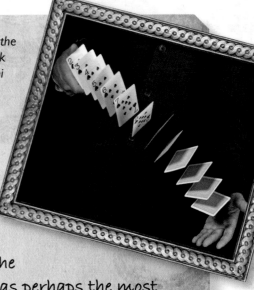

▶ Dai Vernon was one of the few people who could trick the famous Harry Houdini with a card trick.

Fooling Houdini

Magician Dai Vernon (1894–1992) was known as the 'professor'. He was perhaps the most skilful playing-card magician in the history of magic. He even fooled the great Houdini when he performed his trick the 'Ambitious Card'. He repeated the trick eight times and still Houdini could not work out what Vernon was doing!

Coin in pocket

This is one of the most beautiful and graceful coin vanishing tricks used by magicians. It looks simple, but needs lots and lots of practice to make it look convincing to your audience.

Props needed...
* Large coin
* Handkerchief
* Jacket or shirt with a top breast pocket

1

Show your audience the coin you are holding in your left-hand fingertips. Your arm should be stretched out a bit.

2

Drape the handkerchief over the coin but keep hold of the handkerchief with your right hand.

Top Tip!

Find a brightly coloured handkerchief with which to perform the trick. To make your act look really professional, give the handkerchief a good pressing beforehand!

3 Pull the handkerchief across the coin and back towards your breast pocket. The coin can be seen again.

4 Repeat the action, but this time as the handkerchief covers the coin steal it away by gripping it between your right thumb and first finger. The handkerchief will hide the coin from view. Still keep your left hand stretched out as if it still holds the coin.

5 Keep the handkerchief moving backwards towards your breast pocket.

6 As soon as the coin reaches the pocket, just drop it in. Your empty left hand now comes into view. The coin has gone! Toss the handkerchief into the air and show that both of your hands are empty. The coin has completely disappeared!

Elastic arm

How can you make your left arm 30 centimetres longer than your right arm? Just as quickly you change it back to its normal length again, of course!

Preparation

• Wear a short-sleeved shirt or roll up your left shirt sleeve before putting on your jacket.

1 Hold your left arm across your body, pressing it to your chest all the time.

2 Now reach over with your right hand and grab your left wrist and pull it sideways. The hand, of course, moves but the jacket sleeve stays where it was because it is trapped between your left arm and your chest.

3 The illusion of your arm stretching works really well. Try it out in front of a mirror. You can pretend to make your arm shorter again by twisting and pushing it back, still keeping your sleeve trapped as before.